MUSICAL
INSTRUMENTS
Coloring Book

Ellen J. McHenry

DOVER PUBLICATIONS, INC.
New York

Copyright

Bibliographical Note

Musical Instruments Coloring Book is a new work, first published by Dover Publications, Inc., in 1995.

International Standard Book Number

ISBN-13: 978-0-486-28785-0
ISBN-10: 0-486-28785-8

Manufactured in the United States by Courier Corporation
28785810
www.doverpublications.com

Publisher's Note

THE HISTORY OF musical instruments is a spirited, richly detailed, very old story about families. These families are soundmakers that share basic features: how they're made, how they're played, how they sound. Clarinets, for example, are a closely knit family of twelve instruments whose looks, materials, construction, tone colors and playing techniques are related from small instrument to large.

And yet the clarinets are only one part of a far grander family called *woodwinds*, containing such other, smaller, families as recorders, flutes, oboes and bassoons. This story of relatedness is the same for every large musical ensemble. From symphony and jazz orchestras to concert and dance bands, each ensemble is a gathering of specialized soundmakers: woodwinds, brasswinds, brass, percussion, strings, keyboards or plucked instruments.

Over the years, these larger families—also called *sections* or *choirs*—have attracted descriptive labels that aim to capture instrumental personality, a pleasant idea if not taken too seriously. The "glorious, majestic" brass, for instance (trumpets, horns, trombones and so on), are well described. But they can also be raucous, eerie, nasal, funny, explosive, haunting or warmly expressive. Woodwinds have rightly been called the "intimate voices" of the orchestra, but that tag hardly reflects their ear-shattering intensity, perky good humor, lightning speed and flash, or their capacity for great lyricism. And so it goes.

Not every instrument in the world is in this book, but the principal ones of the orchestra and band are here along with a few words about each. For readers as fascinated as we are with the ancient origins of musical instruments, why some have disappeared forever while others are still evolving, take time to look at two books by Anthony Baines: *Woodwind Instruments and Their History*, Dover, 1991 (0-486-26885-3), and *Brass Instruments: Their History and Development*, Dover, 1993 (0-486-27574-4).

The **soprano recorder**'s gentle, soft, flute-like sound is closely associated with music of olden times—courtly Renaissance dances, for example. Evolved from a simple sort of wooden whistle, the medieval instrument grew into a "whole consort" (that is, family) of eight recorders of different size. The larger the instrument, the deeper and richer is its sound.

The wailing, droning cry of the **bagpipe** makes us think of Irish marchers and Scottish pipers; but this strange woodwind was once common throughout medieval Europe. To make it sound, the player inflates the bag through the blow-pipe, then presses on the bag with his left elbow. This sends a steady stream of air to the "chanter" (a pipe with finger-holes, like a recorder) and to the "drones" (each vertical pipe makes its own continuous, one-pitch accompaniment).

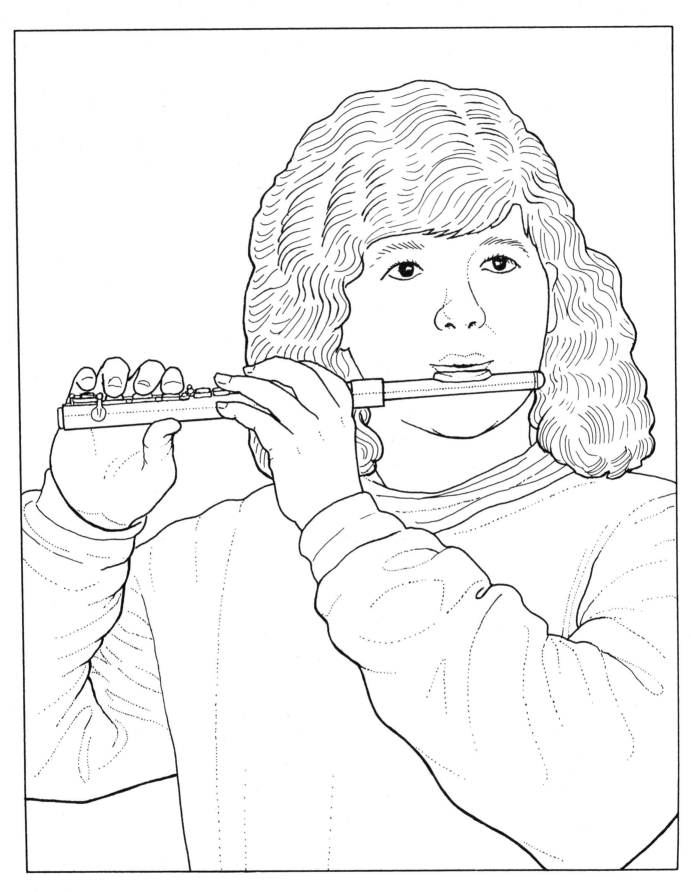

The **piccolo**'s full Italian name is *flauto piccolo*, meaning "little flute." The highest and most agile of all the woodwinds, the piccolo can perform with incredible speed, using its shrill, bright sound—probably the most penetrating in the whole band or orchestra.

At least two or three **clarinets** are part of every symphony orchestra, lending their wide range and expressive sound to the ensemble. But you'll find up to *sixteen* clarinets in concert bands and marching bands! Missing the orchestra's sturdy string section (bands don't have violins, violas or cellos), the band uses the versatile clarinet family as its backbone.

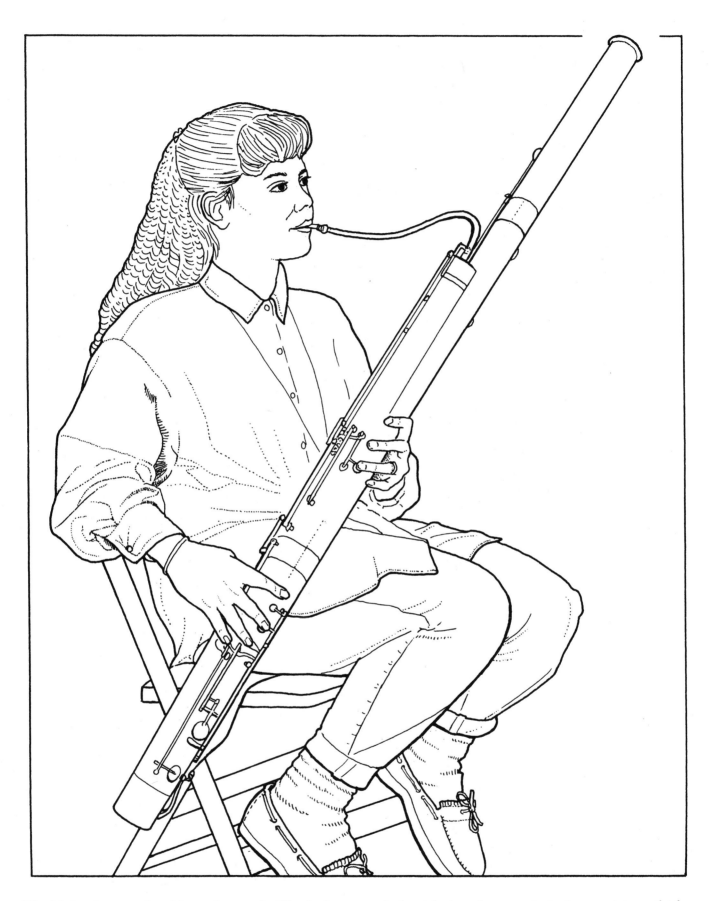

The higher it goes, the thinner it sounds. That's the nature of the **bassoon** as it covers a huge range of *three* octaves. But we always associate this wood-wind with its characteristic *low* register: thick-sounding, rich and a little grumpy.

Spicy and nasal, the **oboe**'s sound can stand out anywhere. This woodwind, made of hardwood from Africa or Brazil, is played by blowing into a "double reed"—two thin strips of cane, tied together, with a wetted opening held between curled lips. Because of their full lungs and tiny exhalation, players say that blowing the oboe feels like swimming under water!

We associate the **flute** with its high, clear, silvery sound. But this descendant of the ancient panpipes can just as easily play breathy, mysterious-sounding melodies in its low register. Made of either wood or metal (even platinum or gold), the flute is played by blowing *across* a side hole—not directly *into* it, like most woodwinds.

With its long body, upturned bell and curve near the mouthpiece, the **bass clarinet** looks more like a saxophone than a clarinet. However, it is a true "big brother" to the traditional clarinet, using the same sort of single-reed mouthpiece and fingerings, but with a much deeper sound. Its bottom notes are extremely dark, almost sinister and mysterious.

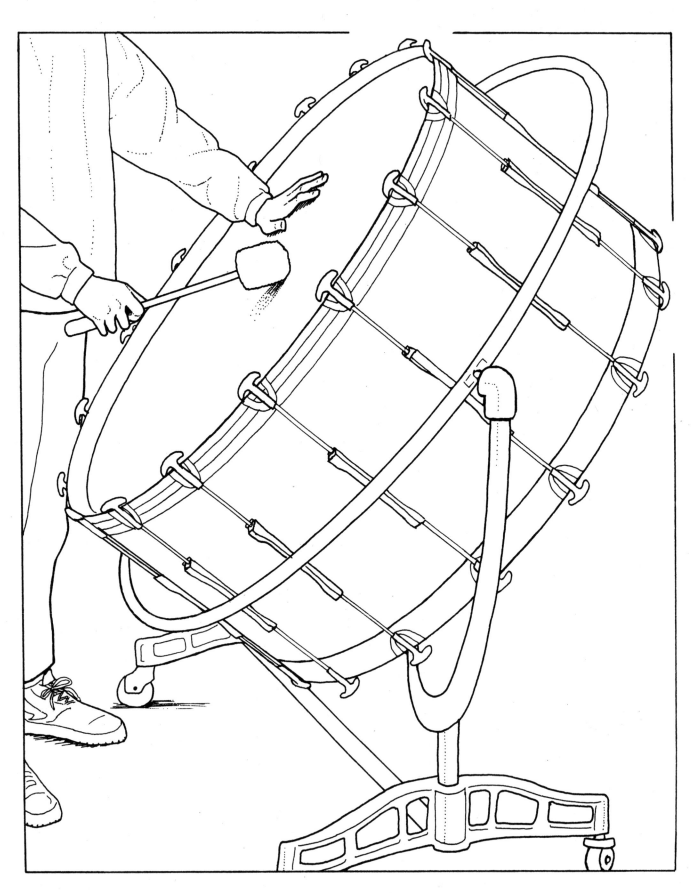

Can the huge **bass drum** play anything besides those rumbling, thunderous *booms* we hear in every marching band? You bet! Using a pair of soft-head beaters—or a double-headed beater played with one hand—the percussionist can play a continuous roll that's almost inaudible, but very mysterious, throbbing and shadowy.

The **snare drum** has a drumhead on top (where the sticks are touching) and another on the bottom (out of sight). Secretly pressing against that bottom head is a tight coil of wire, called a "snare." Want to whack the drum? Then the shock will make the coil vibrate, giving off that special "buzzing" sound of a snare drum. But a hinged off-on release immediately loosens the "snare." Result? A wonderful *tom-tom* sound. No buzz at all!

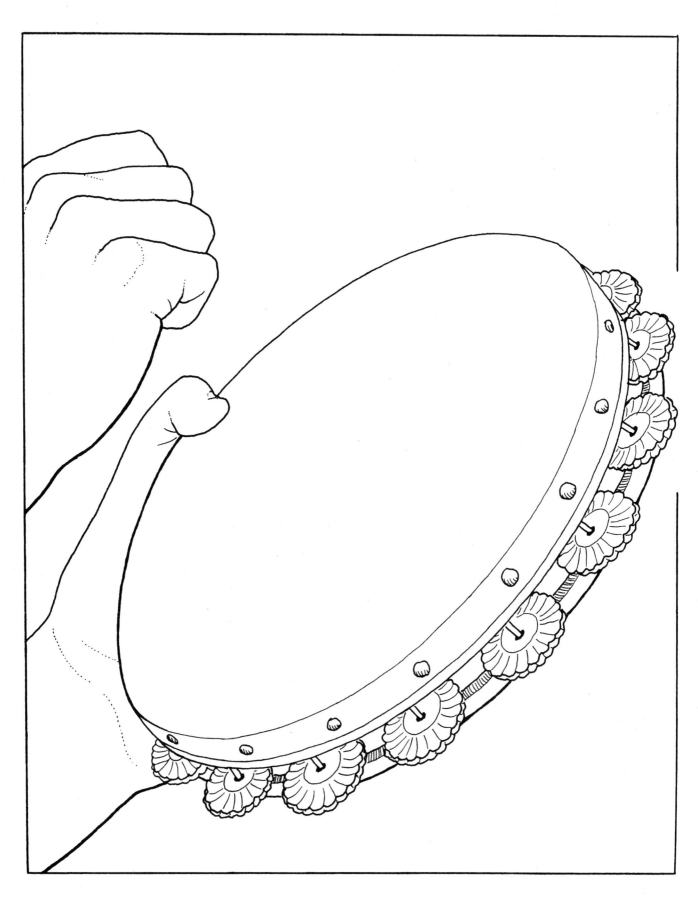

The familiar **tambourine** is usually used to evoke a Neapolitan or Spanish atmosphere. With its metal jingles, it lends a festive feeling to lively dancelike music. Shaking the jingles is only one way to play this percussion instrument. You can strike the drumhead with the fist, rub it with the thumb or tap it with sticks, like any drum.

This ingeniously built instrument is practically a one-person band that contributes a huge amount of percussive punch to the marching band. Called **multi-toms,** sometimes **tim-toms,** these marching drums come in sets of four (called a Quad) or five (a Quint). Made of a tunable head attached to a shell, like a tom-tom or bongo, the drum is struck with a plastic-headed mallet for maximum effect.

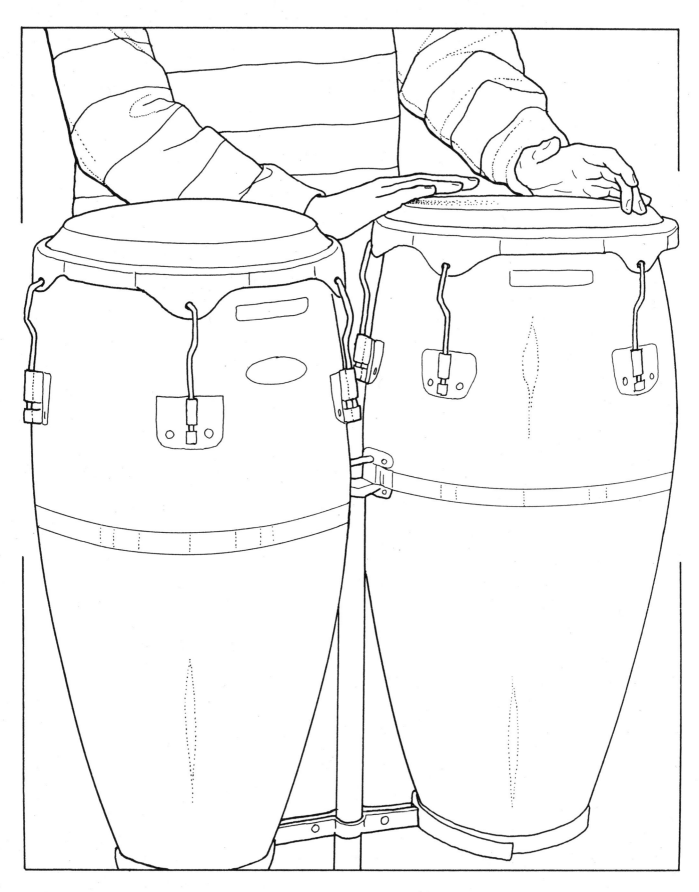

Conga drums, also called *tumbas*, are always played with bare hands, either with the fingers or the flat palm. Because the membranes (drumheads) are very thick and extremely tight, even the lightest touch gives off a resonant sound: deep and rich when struck in the center, higher and brighter when struck near the rim. Conga drums are colorful, important parts of Afro-Cuban music.

16

Early models of the **timpani** or **kettledrum** were hand-tuned by adjusting turnscrews on top of the instrument, near the drumhead. Tuning the modern timpani is faster and easier: by lowering or raising an adjustable footpedal (out of sight in this picture), the player tightens or loosens the drumhead, thereby raising or lowering its pitch. Notice the soft-looking beaters in his hands. They make a quieter sound than sticks with harder tips.

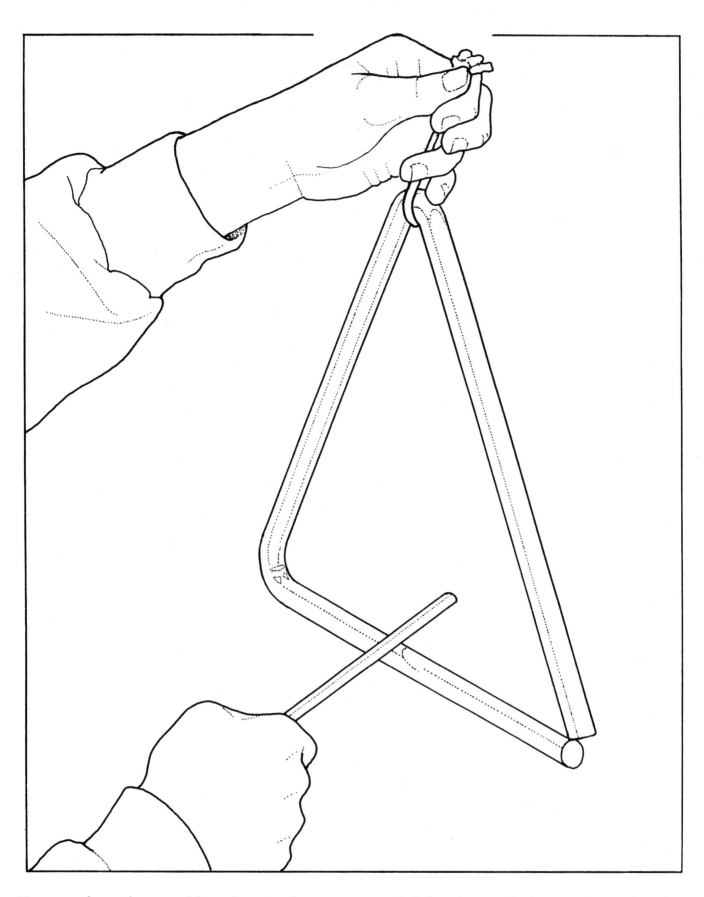

No more than a bent steel bar, the **triangle** produces an astonishing array of very pure, high, brilliant sounds. One laboratory analysis in fact revealed that the sound of a triangle struck with a metal beater was actually a composite of more than *three dozen* separate tones!

The "tuned percussion" instrument played by this young performer is the **tubular bells** or **chimes.** These brass tubes hang in keyboard fashion, like a piano, with the "white" keys (C–D–E, etc.) in front, and the "black" keys (C-sharp, D-sharp, etc.) in the rear. Our player is pressing a "damper" pedal with her foot, quieting, or completely shutting off, the resonating bell sounds she's made with a rawhide hammer.

The popular **crash cymbals** are only part—but the *loudest* part!—of a whole set of cymbals. These "metallophones" (metal soundmakers) range from tiny to huge, and can be played suspended (on a special stand) or hand-held, with a variety of hard and soft beaters.

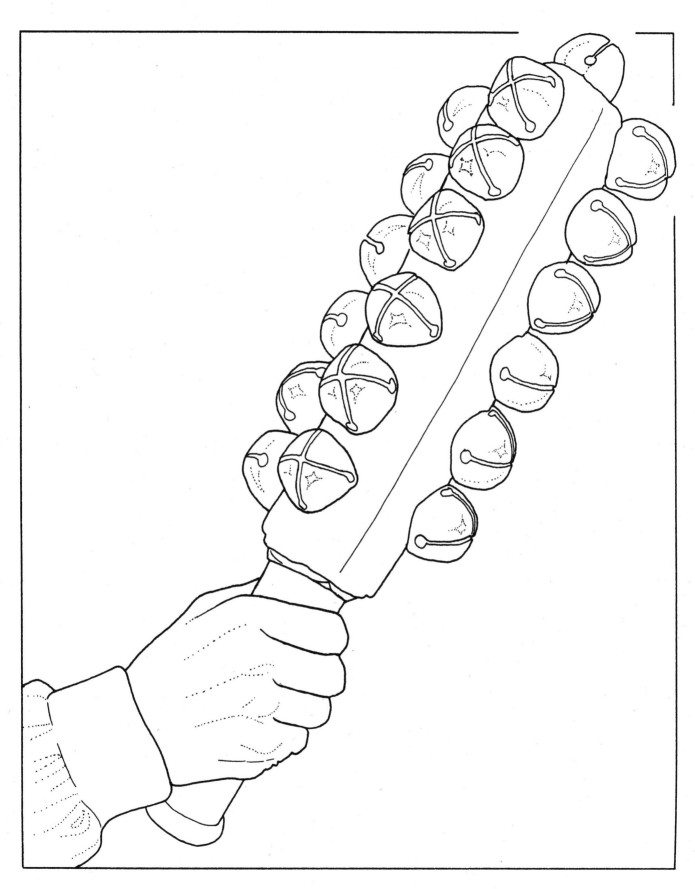

Here are the colorful **sleigh bells** (also called **jingle bells**) that accompany many a Christmas concert. Ever since their arrival in the orchestra in the late eighteenth century, they have been used to imitate the jingle of horse harness-bells, or simply to lend their bright, festive sound to the music.

"Xylon" is the Greek word for *wood*, and "phonê" means *sound*, giving us the familiar **xylophone.** This percussion instrument uses a set of hardwood bars arranged like a piano keyboard. (Our player cleverly handles *four* mallets to play chords with ease.) The crisp, sharp sound of the xylophone is affected by the hardness of the mallet she chooses, but mostly by the resonators seen *under* the instrument. These hollow tubes add a little richness and roundness to the brittle, wooden sound.

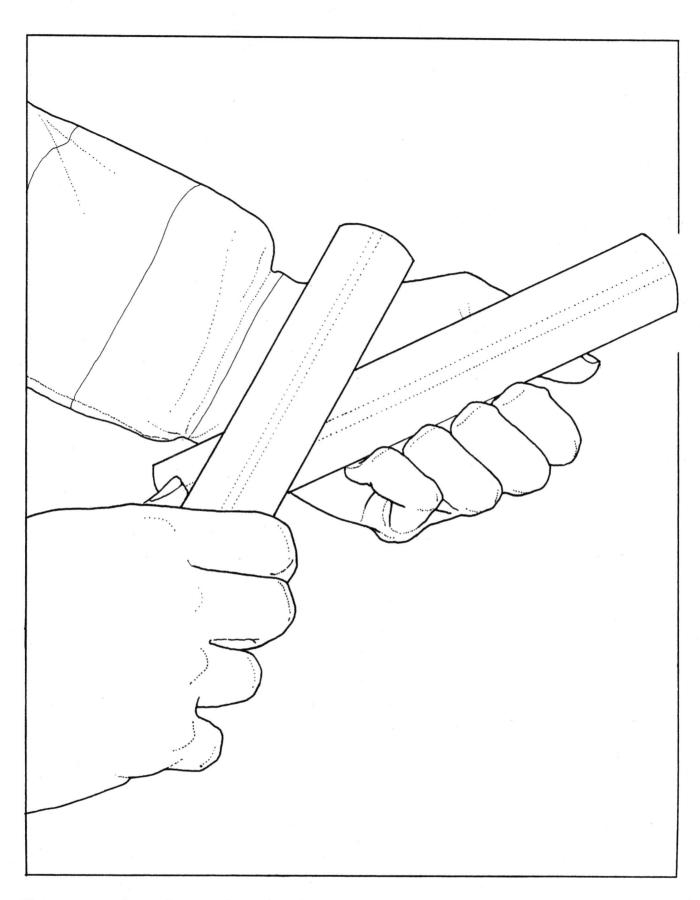

The captivating beat of many Afro-Cuban dances depends on the continuously repeated rhythm of the **claves** (pronounced CLAH-vais). This percussion instrument is usually made of extremely hard Mexican rosewood, creating a penetrating sound as one piece of wood is tapped against the other. In this picture, the player's hollowed left palm acts as a resonator.

"Ensemble" is the French word for *together*—and so they are: families of strings, woodwinds, brass and percussion playing together as an **orchestra** in their annual school concert. As in any good team, each section has its own character and its own role to play. Then, rehearsed and directed by their conductor, they join forces for a common purpose: to make music together. Different ensembles contain different families and varying numbers of players. The *concert band* has no string section. The *marching*

band has no strings and no instruments too cumbersome to march in a parade. The *brass band* has only brass; the *string orchestra*, only strings. The *jazz band* has trumpets and trombones, with saxophones that "double" on other woodwinds, and a small "rhythm section." You'll rarely confuse one ensemble with another. Each has its own character and color: a special ensemble of specialized families.

These familiar Afro-Cuban instruments are the **maracas**—wonderful soundmakers given to us by nature. They were originally made of gourds that were dried in the sun, then emptied. When the dried seeds were put back inside the gourd, they made a dry, rattling sound when the gourd was shaken. Traditional gourd or modern hardwood, the maracas are basic to every Latin-American dance band.

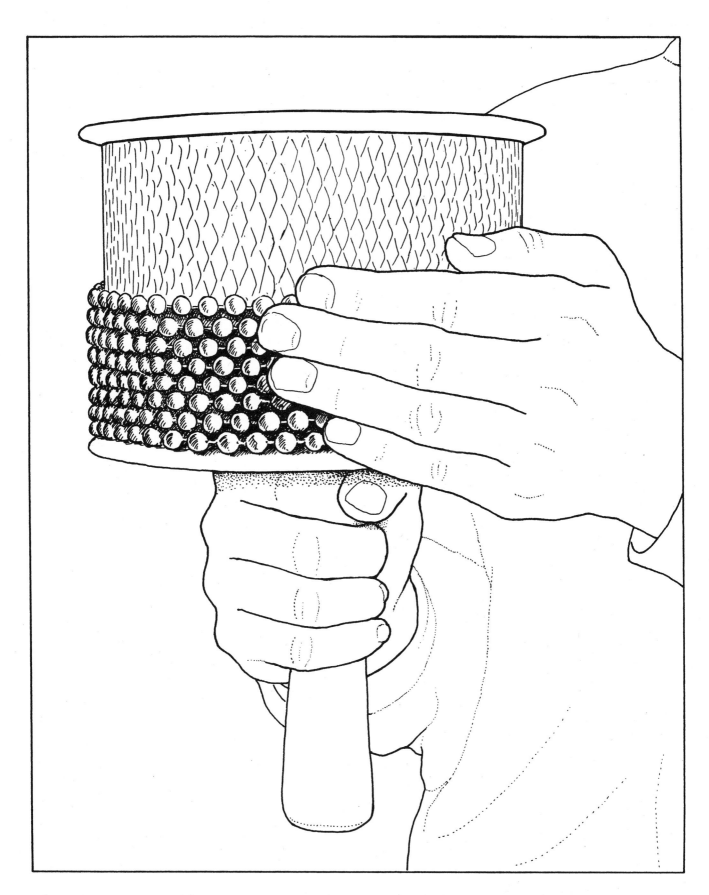

Cabaça (pronounced kah-BAH-sah) is Portuguese for a pumpkin-size gourd. Like the natural maracas, but much larger, the gourd is emptied, dried, then reseeded. But in this case, a net of beads is fitted outside the gourd. The exotic-looking Brazilian instrument in this picture is a modern cabaça, built like a cylinder with an attached handle. By rotating the handle while the left hand holds the beads steady, it produces a *double* sound effect: dried seeds rattling inside . . . and the rattle of beads outside.

The "sax" in *saxophone* is Adolphe Sax, Belgian inventor of this family of instruments; "phonê" means *sound*. With their metal bodies (like brass instruments) and reed mouthpieces (like clarinets), the hybrid saxophones are called "brasswinds." Pictured here is the **alto saxophone.**

This is the **tenor saxophone**—longer and wider than the alto sax shown on the facing page. Both are in-between members of a family of instruments ranging from small (the high-pitched *sopranino* sax) to large and extra-large (the deep-pitched *baritone* and *bass* saxes). This picture shows the sax in a familiar setting, as part of the always-popular marching band.

All saxes, even this large **baritone saxophone,** have exactly the same fingerings (placing the fingers on the keys), although they produce different pitches because of their different sizes. Since all saxes—*and all clarinets as well*—use identical fingerings, a player can easily switch from one instrument to another. Among musicians, the ability to play two instruments is called "doubling."

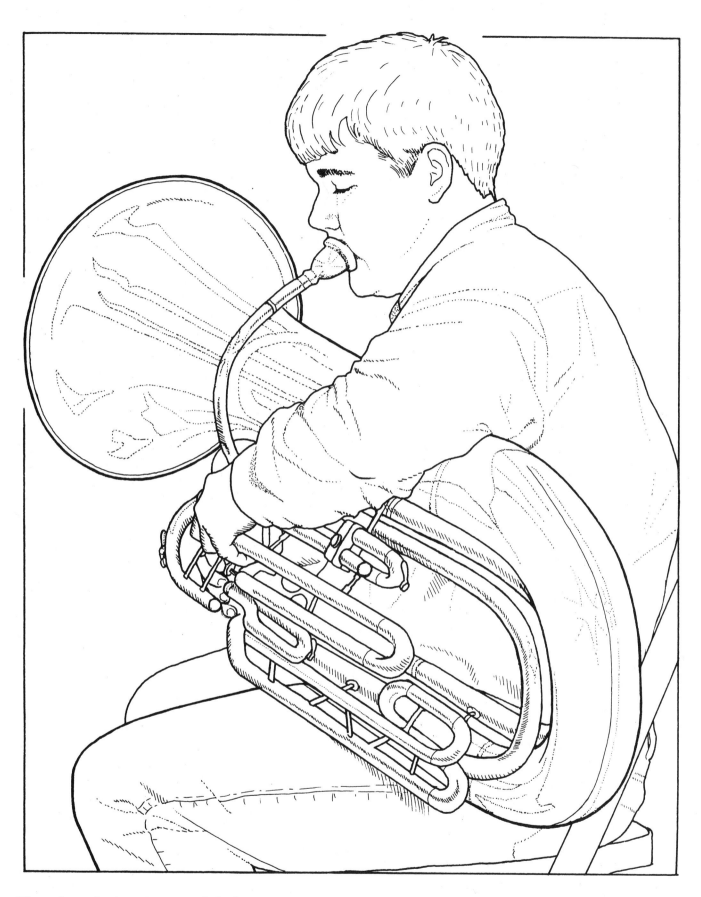

The **tuba** is the bass "voice" of the brass family. To breathe air through its *sixteen* feet of tubing, it's no surprise that the player needs good lungs and a great deal of expelled air to get a sound. In the low register, a single loud note can be sustained for only about four seconds before the red-faced player gives out.

The **baritone horn** may look awkward and unwieldy but is surprisingly agile, with a smooth, warm, mellow tone. The name of the instrument reminds us of how often we refer to instruments in *vocal* terms: *soprano* sax, *alto* clarinet, *tenor* trombone, string *bass*.

The familiar **bugle** call is a daily part of soldiering, from morning *reveille* to evening *taps* . . . and an unforgettable signal for every cavalry charge in "Western" movies! The bugle is the simplest of all the brass instruments, built with only a mouthpiece and a fixed length of tubing. Without valves, it cannot play as many pitches as the trumpet.

Stretched out from end to end, the spiral tubing of the **French horn** is an unbelievable *twelve feet* in length. This versatile instrument—the modern version of the medieval hunting horn—is capable of both brassy fanfares and the most delicate, hushed melody.

Who hasn't dreamed of some day swooping out some brassy sounds by using the **trombone**'s fascinating slide? This part of the instrument (it's detachable, by the way) really does slide, constantly lengthening or shortening the brass tubing—and thus lowering or raising the instrument's pitch.

The huge **sousaphone** is well-known for its *oom-pah* bass notes heard in every marching band. It is actually a bass tuba, curved in a circular form for easier carrying. The bell design of an American variety was suggested by John Philip Sousa, the legendary bandmaster and composer called "The March King." Notice how the bell points forward, sending the sound to the front, in the direction of the march.

How can the **trumpet** produce such a flood of pitches using only three valves? By pushing down one or more valves—those pop-up stems on top of the instrument—the player opens up a special length of trumpet tubing. Then he blows air into it while he tightens his lips in various ways. And out come high notes and low, loud and soft.

Like the sousaphone (see p. 36), the **mellophone** is exclusively a marching-band instrument. With an outward-pointing big bell sending its sound forward, its music always projects in the direction of march. The "voice" of this brass instrument falls somewhere between the sounds of the powerful, robust trombone and the higher, brighter trumpet. Notice the three valves, like the trumpet on the preceding page.

Without a hollow wooden body to amplify their sound, the vibrating strings of the **violin** would be no louder than a plucked rubber band. But those vibrations travel right through the instrument to the air inside its wooden belly, then out, through the "f-holes," to our listening ears. What a lovely sound to enjoy!

The **cello** (pronounced CHEL-o) is the only orchestral stringed instrument that's placed between the seated player's knees. In this comfortable position, the cellist can easily reach the tuning pegs near her face (they're hidden in this picture) to tune the instrument's four strings. The cello is well known for its mellowness, full-bodied low register and its warm, vibrant, singing tone.

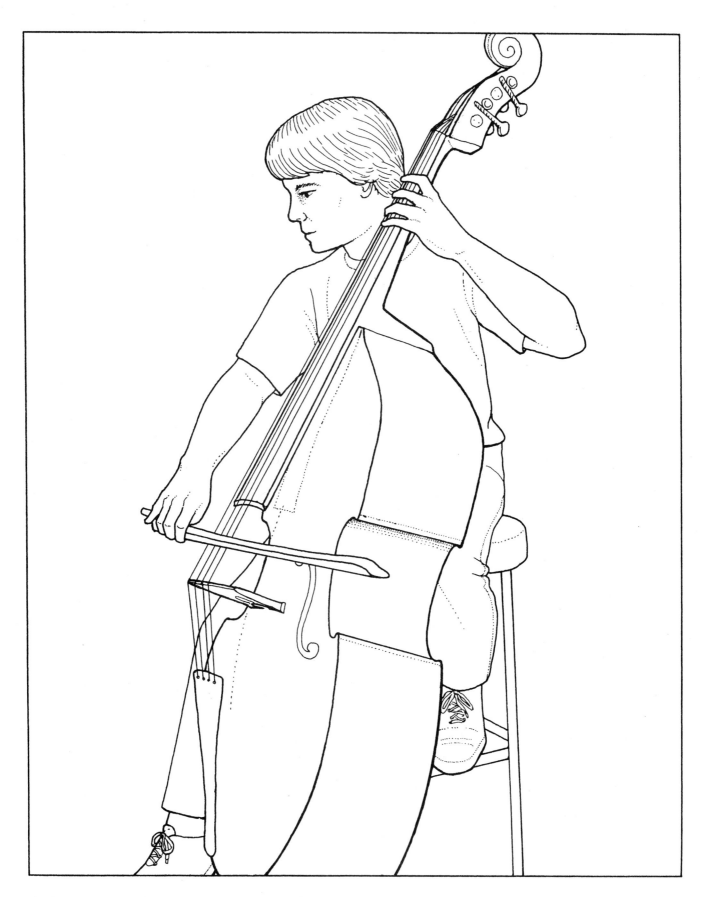

The largest stringed instrument is the **string bass**—
sometimes (in jazz and rock groups) called the
"acoustic bass." Classical music requires players of
all stringed instruments both to bow the strings
and to pluck them (called *pizzicato* in Italian). But for
the string bass, a typical jazz performance prefers
the percussive *snap* of the plucked string. Despite
the size of the instrument, a good player can speed
up and down its long fingerboard with surprising
ease.

The **viola,** like all soundmakers, belongs to a family of instruments with similar features but different sizes. (The smaller instruments sound higher; the larger instruments sound lower.) The viola is somewhat in the middle of its family: above it is the violin; below, the cello and string bass. Larger than the violin, the viola's sound is deeper, darker and richer than the smaller instrument.

The **electric guitar** is the only instrument in our book that's *not* an "acoustical" instrument. Unlike the "folk" guitar, with its resonating hollow body, this guitar has a solid body and electronics to amplify and alter its sound, like a radio or stereo. Its capacity for volume, intensity and special effects has made the electric guitar the most basic and influential instrument in the world of modern popular music.

We think of the **banjo** as a typical American instrument because of its familiar appearance in mountain and Southern folk music. Its roots, however, are distant, probably originating with the African *banju*. The lower hand of this young musician is holding a *plectrum*—a small triangle of ivory, hardwood, metal or plastic used to pluck the tough metal strings.

The **guitar** first appeared in the ancient Orient, but has assumed many different shapes, sizes and names over the centuries. All members of the guitar family—such as the familiar banjo and man- dolin—are stringed instruments that are *always* plucked, *never* bowed (like a violin). The modern guitar is also called by the names "folk guitar" and "acoustic guitar."

Is the **piano** a *percussion* instrument, because we strike its keys with our hands, or a *stringed* instrument, because its sound comes from hammered "strings" (they're actually thick wires) inside the piano? No one has ever decided! In any case, long before the arrival of stereos and TVs, the parlor piano was once the "entertainment center" of many homes as families gathered around it to play and sing.

Ever wonder what's *inside* the **accordion**? Hidden under the player's hands (inside the casings) are many thin, metal reeds. If a stream of air passes over them, the reeds vibrate and make a sound. Our performer pumps up the pleated, hollow bellows, then plays a key or pushes a button to expose certain reeds to the blowing air. Her keyboard is mostly for playing melodies; the buttons activate bass notes and chords.

The **harp** is at least as old as the Bible. Big and small, plain and fancy, this instrument was part of music making in every ancient civilization. Today's "concert grand" harp consists of 47 strings (plucked with both hands *but no little fingers*), a powerful frame with a hollow, wooden sounding board (to amplify the vibrating strings), and seven foot pedals. Why pedals? Not to *sustain* the sound, as you might think, but to *retune* the strings by tightening and loosening them.